Angeliki Koskina and Nikolas Hasanagas

Non-Visual Landscape

Landscape Planning for People with Vision Problems

Angeliki Koskina and Nikolas Hasanagas

NON-VISUAL LANDSCAPE

Landscape Planning for People with Vision Problems

ibidem-Verlag
Stuttgart

Bibliografische Information der Deutschen Nationalbibliothek
Die Deutsche Nationalbibliothek verzeichnet diese Publikation in der Deutschen Nationalbibliografie; detaillierte bibliografische Daten sind im Internet über http://dnb.d-nb.de abrufbar.

Bibliographic information published by the Deutsche Nationalbibliothek
Die Deutsche Nationalbibliothek lists this publication in the Deutsche Nationalbibliografie; detailed bibliographic data are available in the Internet at http://dnb.d-nb.de.

The cover picture is from JR's project: 28 Millimetres, Women Are Heroes - Action in Morro da Providencia, Rio de Janeiro, Brazil - 2008 / Crédit : JR-ART.NET <http://jr-art.net/>. We thank JR for his permission.

∞

Gedruckt auf alterungsbeständigem, säurefreien Papier
Printed on acid-free paper

ISBN-13: 978-3-8382-0196-2

© *ibidem*-Verlag
Stuttgart 2011

Alle Rechte vorbehalten

Das Werk einschließlich aller seiner Teile ist urheberrechtlich geschützt. Jede Verwertung außerhalb der engen Grenzen des Urheberrechtsgesetzes ist ohne Zustimmung des Verlages unzulässig und strafbar. Dies gilt insbesondere für Vervielfältigungen, Übersetzungen, Mikroverfilmungen und elektronische Speicherformen sowie die Einspeicherung und Verarbeitung in elektronischen Systemen.

All rights reserved. No part of this publication may be reproduced, stored in or introduced into a retrieval system, or transmitted, in any form, or by any means (electronic, mechanical, photocopying, recording or otherwise) without the prior written permission of the publisher. Any person who does any unauthorized act in relation to this publication may be liable to criminal prosecution and civil claims for damages.

Printed in Germany

CONTENTS

INDEX OF DIAGRAMS, FIGURES, AND TABLES 7
PREFACE 11
1 INTRODUCTION 15
   1.1 ORIENTATION OF THE RESEARCH 15
   1.2 LITERATURE REVIEW 16
   1.3 AIM OF THE RESEARCH 20
2 METHODOLOGY 23
   2.1 FORMULATION OF THE QUESTIONNAIRE 23
   2.2 COLLECTION OF DATA SAMPLING 24
   2.3 PROCESSING OF DATA 26
3 RESULTS AND DISCUSSION 29
   3.1 THE GENERAL EFFECT OF BLINDNESS ON THE PERCEPTION OF THE LANDSCAPE 29
      3.1.1 SEMIOTIC PERCEPTION 29
      3.1.2 USE OF SENSES 31
      3.1.3 PRINCIPLES OF FUNCTIONALISM 34
      3.1.4 BUILT AND NATURAL ENVIRONMENT 36
      3.1.5 PERCEPTION OF THE LANDSCAPE PHYSICAL CONDITION 39
      3.1.6 PERCEPTION OF MONUMENT VALUES 41
   3.2 SENSES AND PERCEPTION OF LANDSCAPE ELEMENTS 43
   3.3 GENDER EFFECT 46
   3.4 AGE EFFECT 47
   3.5 MARITAL STATUS EFFECT 49
   3.6 EDUCATION LEVEL EFFECT 50
   3.7 EFFECT OF PLACE OF ORIGIN AND RESIDENCE 53
   3.8 EFFECT OF SOCIAL CLASS ON BLIND PEOPLE 55
   3.9 LANDSCAPE TYPOLOGY 58
      3.9.1 SENSES COMBINATION 58
      3.9.2 COMBINATION OF LANDSCAPE ELEMENTS 61

3.9.3 COMBINATION OF FUNCTIONALISM PRINCIPLES...........................65
4 CONCLUSIONS, SUGGESTIONS, AND LIMITATIONS 69
   4.1 CONCLUSIONS 69
   4.2 SUGGESTIONS FOR DESIGNING 74
   4.3 LIMITATIONS AND QUESTIONS FOR FUTURE RESEARCH....................77
SUMMARY...81
REFERENCES 83
APPENDIX.. 93

INDEX OF DIAGRAMS, FIGURES, AND TABLES

DIAGRAMS

Diagram 1. Semiotic perception of landscape 30
Diagram 2. Use of senses 32
Diagram 3. Perception of architectural Functionalism 35
Diagram 4. Perception of landscape elements 37
Diagram 5. Perception of physical landscape condition 40
Diagram 6. Perception of monument values 42

FIGURES

Figure 1. Everton Park Sensory Garden (Liverpool, UK) 20
Figure 2. "Dutch system" for blind people at the campus of Aristotle University of Thessaloniki 53

TABLES

Table 1. Blindness and semiotic perception — 31
Table 2. Blindness and use of senses — 34
Table 3. Blindness and architectural Functionalism — 36
Table 4. Blindness and landscape elements — 39
Table 5. Blindness and physical landscape condition — 41
Table 6. Blindness and monument values — 43
Table 7. Mobilisation of senses in the blind group — 44
Table 8. Mobilisation of senses in the non-blind group — 45
Table 9. Gender effect on the blind group — 47
Table 10. Age effect on the blind group — 48
Table 11. Age effect on the non-blind group — 48
Table 12. Marital status effect on the blind group — 49
Table 13. Effect of education level on the blind group — 51
Table 14. Effect of education level on the non-blind group — 52
Table 15. Effect of place of origin and residence on the blind group — 54
Table 16. Effect of place of origin and residence on the non-blind group — 54
Table 17. Social class and semiotic perception in the blind group — 56
Table 18. Social class and landscape elements in the blind group — 57
Table 19. Interaction of the senses in the blind group — 59
Table 20. Interaction of the senses in the non-blind group — 60
Table 21. Correlations of elements of landscape for the blind group — 62
Table 22. Correlations of elements of landscape for the non-blind group — 64
Table 23. Correlations of Functionalism principles in landscapes for the blind group — 66
Table 24. Correlations of Functionalism principles in landscapes for the non-blind group — 67

PREFACE

In the summer of 2010, the journalist Mr Stavros Theodorakis presented on Greek "Mega Channel" TV (episode 79: "What's the colour of the darkness") the issue of the Thessaloniki School for the Blind, which is in danger of being closed because of financial difficulties. In this episode, many employees and blind people were interviewed.

Mr Theodorakis, having covered his eyes with a sleep mask, was guided by a blind person in the city in order to experience blindness for a few moments. The reportage was quite informative as the blind interviewees "guided" us in the non-visual world. We learnt many things from the programme. "Absence of sight does not necessarily mean absence of personal *vision*." The passages through buildings are discovered by the sound of the walking stick echoing within them. There are only a few shops with the PenFriend or Braille labelling system. Banknotes as well as cooking materials such as oil can be measured with the finger. The dreams of blind people as well as their realities are experienced more "intensively". "Blindness is loneliness." "Touching" the Braille alphabet is a "magical" experience that the non-blind people can never have. A blind person may have difficulties in entering shops with the trained dog. "The pictures of the blind children are composed of sounds, smells, and fantasy." "The education is the eyes of a human-being." A blind man can select a woman for his wife by her voice, perfume, and spontaneous character. "The sound is the most reliable criterion for understanding video content." The music was the only "crack" in the darkness for the musician Ray Charles. And, finally, the blind-born musician Steve Wonder "could not stand this reality even for a minute, if he could see."

The hypothesis that is the basis of and the motivation for this research is that there is not only a real visual landscape. There is also the imaginary visual landscape and four other landscapes – the sound landscape, the smell landscape, the taste landscape, and the touch landscape – all of which address blind people as well. The improvement of blind people's life quality through a careful planning and design of landscape is recognised today as an important social need. These landscapes can also be the subject of a Landscape Architect, as they pertain to the central research interests of Landscape Sociology and the Anthropology of Senses.

Basic prerequisites for the completion of this research were: contact with blind people; the use of the appropriate conceptual tools of Landscape Sociology; and qualitative and quantitative social research methods. This particular analysis was based on semi-structured interviews with blind and non-blind people from a wide range of regions in Greece.

The aim of this work is to provide empirical data for designing landscapes that are appropriate for blind people. Due to the fact that this issue is still unexplored, the goal of this research is not to provide concrete architectural design examples of a landscape for the blind. The goal is to propose standards in statistical terms that can be used as a basis for concrete designs in the future.

We would like to thank Ms G. Leoudi (chairperson of the Blind Association of Xanthi, Greece), Mr P. Karavasilis (chairperson of the National Blind Association of Greece), Mr L. Psalidas (chairperson of the Blind Association of West Thessalia, Greece), Ms M. Bolou (author and ergo-therapist), Ms P. Katsopoulaki, Mr Manolopoulos, Mr A. Tzavaras, Mr Fotopoulos, and all the rest who participated in the present work and who did not want their names to be presented.

Finally, we feel it is an honour and obligation to emphasise the decisive role of the work and the support of Prof. N. Spitalas, Prof. S. Zafiropoulos, Prof. E. Papadopoulou, Prof. A. Styliadis, Prof. M. Ananiadou-Tzimopoulou, Prof. S. Stavridis, Prof. P. Panopoulos, Ms D. Zavraka and Ms E. Polyzou in the development of our discourse in this book.

1 INTRODUCTION

1.1 ORIENTATION OF THE RESEARCH

According to Lawson (2003), a general principle of designed space is to satisfy three basic needs: a) the feeling of security (physical and psychological); b) the feeling of identity (familiarity and identification with the space); and c) the stimulation/attractiveness (arousing interest in the place or offering aesthetic pleasure). An open challenge for the Landscape Architect is to satisfy these three needs in the case of blind people. Apart from the visual landscape, a designer should also take into account the other four landscape types, which come from the other four senses (hearing, smelling, touching, and tasting) (Zavraka 2007; Zafiropoulos 2010). Landscape Sociology and Anthropology of Senses (Panopoulos 2005) deal with these non-visual landscapes. The research has been carried out in the framework of these two fields. However, it has also been based on other areas such as Health Sciences, Environmental Psychology, and Urban Planning.

1.2 LITERATURE REVIEW

The discussion on the necessity to support "top-down" landscape planning through participative "bottom-up" procedures based on "local knowledge" is quite intensive these days (O'Rourke 2005; Stubbs 2008; Hoeppner et al. 2008; Jones 2007; Spirn 2005). Thus, the idea of having planning that will consider the needs of disadvantaged social groups such as the blind is not an idea for a socio-political utopia any more. Thereby, the quantitative social research, which can produce accurate empirical results on this issue, becomes more important.

Ottoson and Grahn (2005) have supported the idea that open spaces have a different impact on the perception of space than do the conditions within the buildings, but they did not examine thoroughly what the individuals perceive. Apart from that, in their insightful work they examined age-specific groups, but not blind people.

Numerous criteria and aspects have been proposed for the visual and non-visual analysis of landscapes such as administrative categories, cohesion, imbalance, historicity, naturalness, etc. (Ode et al. 2008; Tveit et al. 2006). However useful they are for descriptions, they are not so useful for exploring social interactions on the basis of quantitative empirical analysis.

Herrington and Lesmeister (2006) studied the effect of landscape on behaviour, thereby making a great step beyond the superficial visual dimensions of landscape. They focussed on children, however, and not on blind people. Their work enlightened ideas about behavioural aspects but it disregarded the determinants of landscape perception.

Read (2005) attempted a thorough study on the perception of various landscape types such as the "rural", the "aesthetic", and the "picturesque" landscapes. He was mainly interested in the polarisation of beliefs and values among certain social groups ("local" or "foreign", experts or laypersons) and not in proposing what factors draw their attention. He provided an analysis of a political issue rather than a sociological approach to human-space relations and did not focus on blind people or on the non-visual dimensions of landscape.

Moore-Colyer and Scott (2005) referred to the existence of non-visual dimensions of the landscape. They recognised the role of the "rural" landscape as a "taste landscape" in the beginning of 20th century for several urban groups that constituted the "élite", which admired the products it provided. Thereby, they proposed a promising path of exploring non-visual dimensions of a landscape. However, they mainly observed the historical development of local values and did not extend the analysis to further details about how a landscape is perceived.

Kim et al. (2008) and Doevendans et al. (2007) connected the aesthetic with the ecological dimensions of a landscape. These dimensions are analysed in the present book as principles of architectural Functionalism. The relationship between them is confirmed by the quantitative results.

Thwaits et al. (2005) examined how spatial experiences affect the emotions, but they analysed the spatial experience in three abstract dimensions: "local", "directional", and "transitional". This abstract approach is useful for the understanding of psychological processes rather than for the exploration of the attitudes of specific social groups towards space and how they perceive it. Thus, this approach can hardly be directly functional for a landscape designer.

In a review of the proceedings of the Symposium of the Association of American Geographers, which was carried out in 2007 and was entitled "Geographies of Disability", Crook et al. (2008) recognised a tendency of many researchers to focus on issues related to impacts of chronic diseases, to technology, and to social inclusion (Holt 2003, Hall and Kearns 2001). However, their research was oriented to individuals with hearing problems, and persons with mental and other diseases, but not to blind people.

Researchers who extensively examined the relation between gender and space (Chen et al. 2008; Coluccia et al. 2007) focussed on questions about orientation ability and not on the ability to perceive landscape elements and features. The role of urban green zones in the perception of landscapes was examined at the functional and semiotic levels in an innovative approach, but did not focus on blindness (Smardon 1988).

Espinosa et al. (1998) provided interesting results concerning the ability of the blind to orientate themselves by touching maps, but they did not go into deep detail concerning the environmental features they perceived.

Carles et al. (1992) thoroughly dealt with the analysis of non-visual landscapes and, in particular, of "soundscapes". They combined four "natural" and "semi-natural" sounds with eight visual landscapes and measured the preferences of pupils for these.

The results showed that the differences within the sounds had a stronger influence on their preferences than the differences in the visual landscapes. They also discovered that there was a preference for natural sounds such as birds and water, while the attitudes towards less recognisable sounds, such as insects, were not statistically significant. However, the results of this research did not support this, either in the case of blind or in the case of non-blind individuals. Hedfords and Berg (2003) also explored the role of the "soundscape" in the creation of identity but without providing very concrete and generalisable quantitative results in their innovative analysis.

In addition, despite the importance of touching in perceiving an environment (Bolou and Gkouveris 2000), according to the results of this research, it seems that the sense of touch functions dispersedly and is not focussed on certain types of local elements. However, this could be considered to be a confirmation of its importance, since its dispersed function means that it is applicable to a wide range of landscape elements.

Remarkable attempts have been made in order to create gardens that can satisfy emotional needs in addition to providing visual aesthetics. These are the so-called "sensory gardens". These are supposed to be appropriate for individuals with special needs, including blind people (websites 2, 3, 4, 5, 7, 8, 9, 10, 11). A prominent example is the case of Everton Park Sensory Garden (Figure 1), which aims at stimulating all five senses and making the impression of "travelling" in the world of the senses.

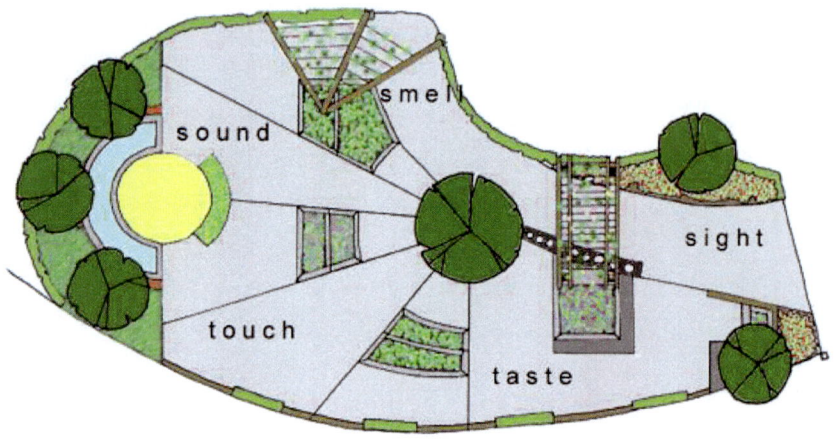

Figure 1. Everton Park Sensory Garden (Liverpool, UK)

For that purpose, it uses plants of different textures, smells, tastes, as well as water (website 1). However, these gardens were designed through artistic inspiration and did not use empirical data concerning the perception of non-visual landscapes. Progress has been made in designing gardens for blind people, but only while regarding security measures and facilities for people with vision problems, and not regarding the perception of the landscapes themselves (website 6).

1.3 AIM OF THE RESEARCH

The main question we are trying to answer is: What basic prerequisites should be ensured for the design of a landscape for blind people so as to provide a safe, familiar, and attractive environment? The sub-questions are the following: a) How do blind people perceive the landscape from a semiotic viewpoint? b) What senses do they employ? c) What principles of architectural

Functionalism do they pay attention to? d) What are the landscape elements they perceive? e) What physical situations do they perceive? g) What monument (memorial) values might they maintain? A control group of non-blind individuals has been used in order to make the statistical differences between blind and non-blind people clearer. Considering the lack of necessary quantitative empirical data in the international literature that would change the architectural design from an artistic one to a more scientific one, the present research is purposeful.

The term "planning" in this analysis is not meant as "design". This is not possible because this research issue is still quite unexplored. This would be possible only in future research that is based on these quantitative results. In this analysis, with the term "planning" we mean the standards, ideas, and suggestions that are derived from the quantitative results and can constitute a conceptual framework that can be used by a designer for more rational, strategic decision-making in any spatial intervention.

2 METHODOLOGY

At first, extensive in-depth interviews were conducted. The text was then analysed on the basis of a conceptual categorisation. The concepts were borrowed from the fields of the socio-semiotics, architectural Functionalism, etc., as described in section 2.3.

2.1 FORMULATION OF THE QUESTIONNAIRE

The basic principle for forming the questionnaire was the hypothesis that a landscape is the subjective impression derived from a place (Eleftheriadis 2008, Hasanagas 2007). Thus, a place can be perceived in various ways (each observer pays attention to different landscape elements) and at various dimensions (different values and functions of a place can be regarded as important by different observers). The way the landscape is recorded depends on one's culture and idiosyncrasies, which constitute the "filter of perception" (Meining 1979). Different observers may see "tranquility", "abandonment", or "nostalgia" at the same park. Also, an observer may be interested in the monuments of the park, while another observer can be interested only in the fauna, etc.

On the basis of this hypothesis, we formulated a questionnaire with 26 questions. Five of these concerned personal data (age, marital status, education level, profession, self-assessment of social status). The remaining 21 questions focussed on the experiences and preferences of the interviewees so as to explore their filters of perception. Dimensions of landscape perception that were suggested in the literature (Ode et al. 2008; Tveit et al. 2006; Meining 1979; Botton 2008) were operationalised in the first version of questionnaire, which was improved after five trial interviews with blind people. These five interviewees were interviewed again with the questions that were added. The 21 questions have to do with: 1) the landscape that prevails in fantasy; 2) the landscape of childhood as specified by the interviewees themselves and by witnesses they have heard; 3) general relation between the landscape and recreation; 4 and 5) recreation landscape; 6 and 7) relation between landscape and music; 8) relation between landscape and taste; 9) relation between landscape and socialisation; 10) unpleasant landscape; 11, 12, 13, 18, 19, and 21) desirable landscape; 14) ecological dimension at a micro-level (house garden); 15 and 16) ecological dimension at a macro-level (park); 17 and 20) landscape of social organisation.

2.2 COLLECTION OF DATA SAMPLING

The particular sample is, and should be, a judgement sample. It was selected in a way that involves individuals of various ages, different education levels, and different degrees of social class consciousness so as to illustrate more clearly the effects of these factors on landscape perception.

The sample contains 294 cases of landscape perception by the blind interviewees (294 = 14 interviewees * 21 questions) and 294 cases of landscape perception by the control group of the non-blind interviewees, respectively. We examined a total of 588 cases. It is important to clarify that these cases are not about individuals but cases of landscape perception. This is not an artificial inflation of case numbers, since it is obvious that every individual imagines different landscapes for different circumstances (e.g., one may wish to be in a big city for his honeymoon and in a coastal village for a family excursion). In addition, the consideration of the same physical subject as "several different cases", since it is characterised by different reactions and various identities under different circumstances, is an acceptable approach in quantitative social research (Hasanagas 2004).

The interviews were conducted by telephone of the 14 blind people (not since birth) and 14 non-blind people. The basic difficulties were: a) the refusal for cooperation of certain blinds associations; and b) the hesitation of free expression in the case of some interviewees. The first difficulty caused delays but it did not affect the final quality of the results. The second difficulty was overcome by the argument that this research has a purely scientific purpose and the interviewees would remain anonymous.

The sample of 14 blind people included: 3 women and 11 men, from 26 to 74 years old (mean=54). Nine of them were married and 2 were university degree holders (humanities). They were working in the primary, secondary, and in the tertiary sectors of the economy (e.g., stockbreeding, crafts industry, and commerce). Their residences were in southern Greece (Rethimno in Crete, Kalamata in Peloponnesus), central Greece (Athens), and northern

Greece (Thessaloniki, Xanthi, Paranesti, Trikala, Pyli). They were born in southern Greece (Kalamata and Meligala in Peloponnesus, Rethimno in Crete), central Greece (Viotia, Trikala), and northern Greece (Giannitsa, Kavala, Chalkidiki, Paranesti).

The sample of the 14 non-blind individuals included: 3 men and 11 women, from 22 to 87 years old (mean=43). Six of them were married and 11 were university degree holders (positive sciences and humanities). They were working in the tertiary sector (e.g., commerce, bookkeeping). Their residences were in southern Greece (Patra, Kalamata and Mani in Peloponnesus), central Greece and the islands (Athens, Siros), and northern Greece (Drama, Paranesti, Nea Zichni). They all were born in the same areas they lived in.

Between these groups, there is an evident disproportional and inverted distribution of certain variables such as gender and education levels. This is not expected to affect the results because of the large number of heterogeneous cases (588 cases). Apart from that, the variables that are supposed to influence the number and the quality of landscape perceptions – namely the age and the place of residence and birth – are not disproportionally distributed between the two groups.

2.3 PROCESSING OF DATA

A bivariate analysis (Pearson test) was conducted at significance level of $p<0.01$ (**) and $p<0.05$ (*) after normality control with the tests of Kolmogorv-Smirnov and Shapiro-Wilk. To get a sense of social status, a two-step cluster was carried out because the Pearson test could not detect the dependencies.

- Independent variables

The education level was measured on a binary scale (0= not a university graduate, 1= university graduate). Social status was measured with a three-grade scale (1= low, 2= middle, 3= upper). The size of the residential area and place of birth were measured on a three-grade scale (3= Athens or Thessaloniki, 2= capital of prefecture, 1= other). The age of the interviewees was measured in metric scale.

- Dependent variables

The text of the interviews was analysed quantitatively by means of a classification system based on concepts of Landscape Sociology (Hasanagas 2007) and Socio-semiotics of Space (Stavridis 1990), of architectural Functionalism (Nikolaidou 1993), of the Monument Theory (Riegl 1982), and of Landscape Management and Analysis (Spitalas 2003, Ananiadou-Tzimopoulou 1992, Styliadis et al. 2008, Vyzantiadou et al. 2007, Eleftheriadis 2008, Dimen and Palamariu 2007, Dzitac and Valeanu 2007, Hasanagas et al. 2010). In particular, the following variables were graded on a binary scale (0= not present, 1= present)

Variables of semiotics:

1) Icon (the signifier is identical with the signified, e.g., a simple rock, which as seen in the interview is not related to anything); 2) Trace (outcome of human action, e.g., a bench);

3) Index (the signifier is related to the signified with a functional-existential relationship, e.g., Aristotle Square, which functions as a central point for socialising and economic activity in Thessaloniki and signals the city itself or the White Tower of Thessaloniki, which was a fortress necessary for the existence of the city: both of them exist because Thessaloniki exists); 4) Symbol (the signifier is arbitrarily related with the signified and means a solution or danger, e.g., religious symbols); 5) Metaphors (parallelism with an homologous situation, e.g., flavour of meat that reminds one of Easter).

Variables of senses (elements of landscapes that activate the relevant senses, e.g., aromatic flowers for smell, walking on pebbles for touch).

Variables of architectural Functionalism (work, entertainment, transport, aesthetics, ecology, social organisation, and socialisation).

Character of landscape elements: 1. built environment; 2. natural environment: i) flora that is analysed in low and high vegetation, coniferous, broad-leaved, aromatic and decorative plants; and ii) fauna that is separately examined for mammals and birds.

Physical conditions of landscape: 1. geo-morphology, e.g., sand, plain, mountain; 2. water; 3. air and sky, e.g., clouds, sunset.

Monument values: 1. historical value: information about the past; 2. age-value, namely nostalgia.

3 RESULTS AND DISCUSSION

3.1 THE GENERAL EFFECT OF BLINDNESS ON THE PERCEPTION OF THE LANDSCAPE

3.1.1 SEMIOTIC PERCEPTION

In Diagram 1 we see that the landscape perceived by both non-blind people and blind individuals presents similar semiotic synthesis. The icons constitute the greatest part of the semiotic synthesis of the landscape, the traces play a secondary role, symbols hold the third position, metaphor is less dominant, and the indexes are almost non-existent. It is evident that the perception of icons is the simplest approach to reality and this is preferable for both groups. Only a few are willing to adopt complex representations of the reality, such as indexes or symbols, which create an alternative semantic level. Thereby, a landscape designer should not expect blind individuals to be more impressed by an index or a symbol (e.g., monument, national plant) due to their possible needs for alternative realities. The simple design is suitable for both the blind individuals and the non-blind people.

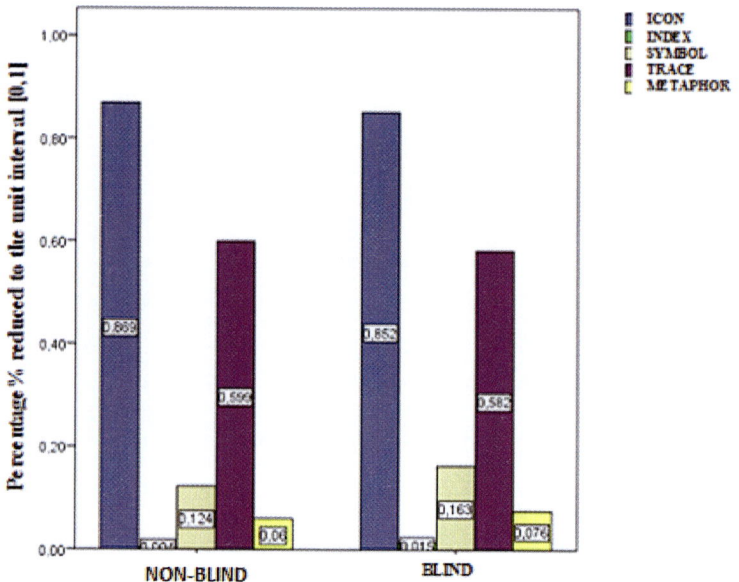

Diagram 1. Semiotic perception of landscape

Indeed, this independence between the factor of blindness and semiotic perception is also confirmed by the statistical analysis in Table 1. In this table, it seems that, in general, blind people are not differentiated from non-blind people as far as semiotic perception is concerned. Their landscapes involve almost the same number of icons, indexes, symbols, traces, and metaphors. So the blind individuals do not present a stronger need for acquiring landscape experiences – even imaginary ones – than the non-blind people, as might be expected. The landscape imagination is not a substantial reaction against blindness. If it was, then the blind people would imagine landscapes with more indexes or symbols (of visual character or not) that would cite alternative, wider range of reality fields, e.g., Aristotle Square, which is an index for the whole city of

Thessaloniki, or sweet taste, which is a symbol of celebrations, anniversaries, Christmas, etc.

Table 1. Blindness and semiotic perception

	BLINDNESS
ICON	-.033
	.441
INDEX	.059
	.176
SYMBOL	.055
	.203
TRACE	.005
	.913
METAPHOR	.032
	.462

3.1.2 USE OF SENSES

In the descriptive statistics (Diagram 2), the contribution of senses to the perception of the landscape seems to be similar for blind individuals and non-blind people. Vision seems to play an important role in both groups (in the case of the blind group, it is of course an imaginary vision). Thus, a designer should take into account that the blind group may continue to activate their vision through use of their imaginations when they visit, e.g., a park and they will not necessarily be satisfied only with touching (e.g., small vegetation) or hearing (e.g., breeze in the leaves).[1]

In both groups, the classification is as follows: vision appears to play the most important role, touching comes second, hearing

---

[1] Of course, one should overlook the fact that the blind sample in this research does not include people born blind but blind people with past visual experience.

comes third, and taste and smell hold the last positions. A natural difference is that in non-blind people, the contribution of vision is much higher than with the remaining senses, while in the blind individuals, (imaginary) vision contributes to the perception of the landscape just a little more than hearing and touching. Smell and taste seem to be atrophic in both groups. Therefore, if items for smell or taste are used in a landscape design, they can hardly make it more successful, even if they look "innovative" (e.g., smell of sea, farm smell). If a designer is going to use non-visual means, he/she has more chances of being successful by using elements that stimulate senses of touch and hearing.

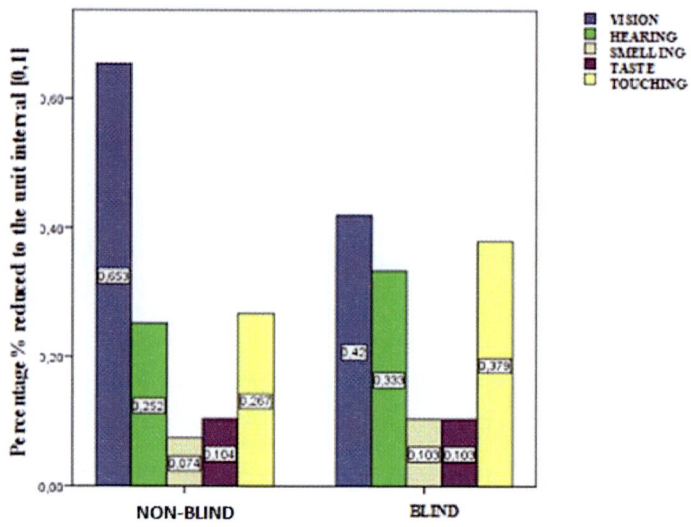

Diagram 2. Use of senses

As expected, vision plays a prominent role in the perception of landscape by non-blind people, while in the case of the blind group, it contributes to the perception of the landscape in synergy with touching and hearing (Table 2). The landscape of the blind, as expected, is constructed by touching elements (grass, sand at the beach, obstacles in the street, sand that is dry and makes a blind person feel secure enough to run) rather than through imaginary vision. However, it should be emphasised that the relevant statistical coefficients, even though significant, are relatively weak (-0.234 for vision and 0.120 for touching). Also, the landscape elements that stimulate the remaining senses (hearing, smell, taste) do not present a statistically significant difference between the blind and the non-blind people groups. Touching is proven to be the second most important sense after vision for perceiving a landscape, as touch recognition of an object is the clearest one, while smell, taste, and hearing are not used by the blind individuals more extensively than with the non-blind people, even though there are many enjoyments in life based on these three senses. In addition, the psychological hypothesis that imagination is developed through vision and touch, while it remains atrophic in the remaining three senses, is supported by these findings. Indeed, many people can compose their own visual and touching imaginations but only a few (e.g. experienced cooks, perfumers, musicians) can invent new, original tastes, smells or music and sounds.

Table 2. Blindness and use of senses

	BLINDNESS
VISION	-.234(**)
	.000
HEARING	.089
	.085
SMELL	.051
	.320
TASTE	-.001
	.987
TOUCHING	.120(*)
	.020

3.1.3 PRINCIPLES OF FUNCTIONALISM

In Diagram 3, the need for socialising is of prominent importance in the perception of landscapes by non-blind people and blind people. A landscape designer should take under consideration that loneliness is not a characteristic of blind people. Thus, they would not accept a landscape with no possibility for socialisation (e.g., conditions that facilitate moving and transport).

However, in order to set acceptable priorities for the blind, the socialisation should be separated from the aesthetics and recreation. Particularly, it must be taken into account that though the needs for recreation and aesthetics are almost equivalent with the need for socialisation in the landscapes of non-blind people, blind individuals rank the other functions lower compared to socialisation (e.g., for blind people, it is often more important to assure access to their association than access to a park).

A function that appears to be of equal importance between the non-blind people and the blind is the ecological dimension of the landscape (e.g., vegetation). The issue of residence seems to be of greater importance for the blind individuals because of their more "static" condition. The need for a landscape that facilitates transport is a necessity for both groups. The need for a landscape that creates attractive working conditions is not so important for the blind group.

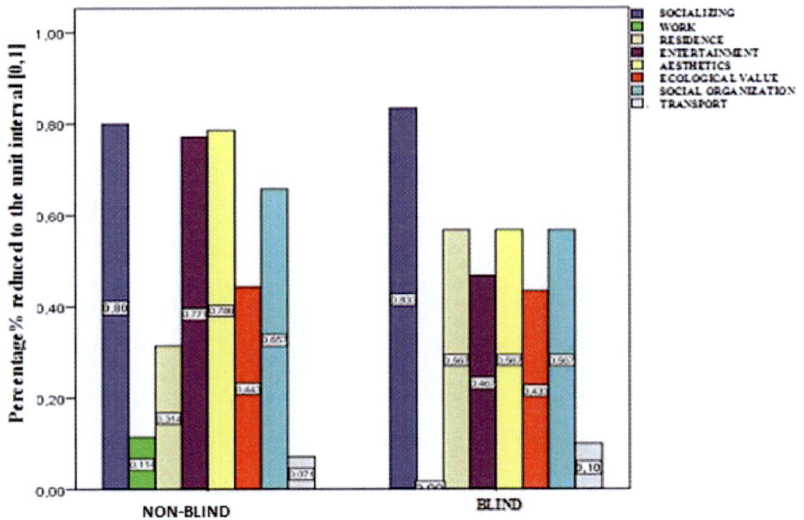

Diagram 3. Perception of architectural Functionalism

In Table 3, we see that from the four basic principles of architectural Functionalism (work, residence, entertainment, transport), residence is of great importance, while aesthetics are of least importance for the blind. This is understandable, as the accessibility of any other place from the residence is of crucial importance in the everyday lives of blind individuals.

The fact that aesthetics are of minor value for the blind group can be attributed to their preference to stay at home due to the lack of access to a wide range of places. Under such conditions, it is understandable that the aesthetic value of the wider "reality" is regarded as "secondary" or even as a utopia. Other landscape functions such as socialisation, attractive working conditions, recreation, transport, and respect for the natural environment are as important for the blind individuals as for the non-blind people.

Table 3. Blindness and architectural Functionalism

	BLINDNESS
SOCIALISATION	-.093
	.221
SOCIAL ORGANISATION	-.011
	.800
WORK	-.043
	.338
RESIDENCE	.141(**)
	.002
ENTERTAINMENT	-.023
	.609
AESTHETICS	-.155(**)
	.000
ECOLOGIC VALUES	-.008
	.855
POSSIBILITY OF TRANSPORT	.044
	.384

3.1.4   BUILT AND NATURAL ENVIRONMENT

A designer should consider the fact that the built and the natural environment play a significant role for the blind and the non-blind people (Diagram 4). However, the designer should not think that the blind are especially demanding concerning the types of planting materials. Thus, not much time should be spent on a detailed examination of the blind's preferences for planting materials. In contrast to non-blind people, who pay attention to various details of the vegetation, the blind do not have any particular preferences concerning the type of plants (e.g., high or low vegetation), though one would expect that they would prefer grass for smooth walking and fewer trees for safety reasons. So, planting materials may be an important dimension of the landscape as perceived by the blind, but it is quite abstract.

However, in designing landscapes for the blind, emphasis should be given to the existence of animals, as they should be present in abundance (especially mammals and birds).

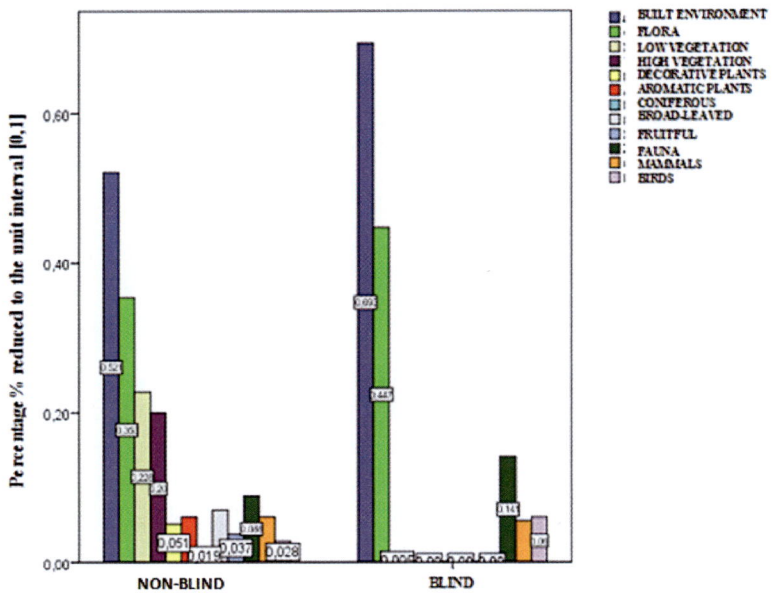

Diagram 4. Perception of landscape elements

In Table 4, in particular, we notice that the built landscape dominates blind people's realities, while plants are of secondary importance. This can be attributed to the difficulties they feel regarding access (difficulty of accessing central squares in cities, difficulty of crossing pavements because of parked bicycles and cars and other obstacles, etc). It is statistically supported that a green environment may acquire a positive essence in the blind's conscience, yet, all of its elements (low and high vegetation, decorative and aromatic plants, conifers and broad-leaved trees, etc) are disregarded with negative or weak statistical numbers in the landscape as perceived by the blind. In contrast to non-blind people, an appropriately built environment is a necessity for the blind, while a green environment with rich vegetation is rather a luxury for them.

As far as the fauna is concerned, neither mammals nor birds appear more intensively in the landscapes of the blind, though these elements become distinct through hearing or touching. Apparently, despite their distinct presence in Diagram 4, they should be considered by the designer as decorative features rather than as necessities. The perception of a green environment is generally strong.

Table 4. Blindness and landscape elements

	BLINDNESS
STRUCTURED	.174(**)
	.000
VEGETATION	.098(*)
	.045
LOW	-.335(**)
	.000
HIGH	-.322(**)
	.000
DECORATIVE PLANTS	-.156(**)
	.001
AROMATIC PLANTS	-.171(**)
	.000
CONIFEROUS	-.094
	.056
BROAD-LEAVED	-.184(**)
	.000
FRUIT-BEARING PLANTS	-.133(**)
	.007
FAUNA (GENERAL)	.087
	.073
MAMMALS	-.008
	.876
BIRDS	.082
	.094

3.1.5 PERCEPTION OF THE LANDSCAPE PHYSICAL CONDITION

In the landscape of non-blind people, water plays a significant role (e.g., sea), while the land-related geomorphologic features (such as mountains) come in second place with a minor difference (Diagram 5). Compared to water and land, air- and sky-related features (e.g., sunset) receive little attention. In the blind, both land and water contain distinguishable features, while air- and sky-related features receive little attention (e.g., clouds, sunset). Therefore, the designer should know that although the water elements may easily impress non-blind people, they are not so impressive for the blind people. In the case of blind landscape users, the designer should maintain a balance between these two elements of nature (water and land). In addition, the designer should not forget that possible weaknesses in the usage of these specific features can not be outweighed by air- or sky-related features. The air- and sky-related features can only be perceived by the blind visitors as a reflection created, e.g., during an excursion in a natural area.

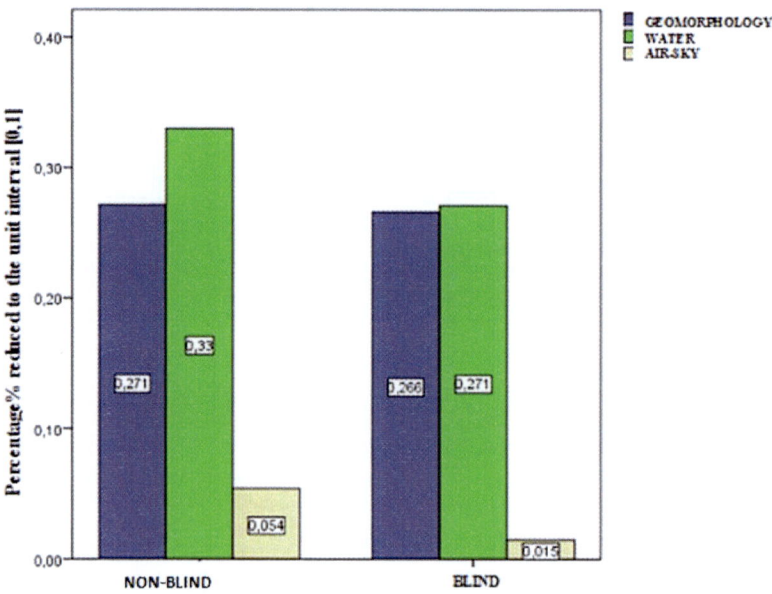

Diagram 5. Perception of physical landscape condition

However, a designer should be aware of the fact that land and water features do not have a significant influence in the perception of landscapes by non-blind people and the blind (Table 5). Air- and sky-related features are almost absent from blind people's landscapes. In the case of non-blind people, though, these features seem to be more stimulating, since they are strongly related to vision. Water and anaglyphic characteristics of land appear in the landscapes of non-blind people and the blind to a similar degree, since in both elements touching is dominant, especially in the blind group (see Table 2).

Table 5. Blindness and physical landscape condition

	BLINDNESS
GEOMORPHOLOGIC	-.004
	.928
WATER	-.064
	.190
AIR- AND SKY-RELATED ELEMENTS	-.105(*)
	.031

3.1.6   PERCEPTION OF MONUMENT VALUES

In Diagram 6, age and historical value influence to a limited degree the perception of landscape by non-blind people, since more recent landscape experience is for them of greater importance. In particular, historical value has almost no impact on the non-blind people. The blind, on the contrary, live with memories and reflections from the past. Thus, the designer of landscapes for the blind can use auxiliary features that remind them of the past (e.g., island songs with an artificial sea odour; aromatic wild plants with songs from mountainous villages; aromatic, low, garden vegetation). Of course, if the designer decides to incorporate such features, then these should be of a large variety and combined in various patterns in order to cover a wide range of expectations and personal experiences.

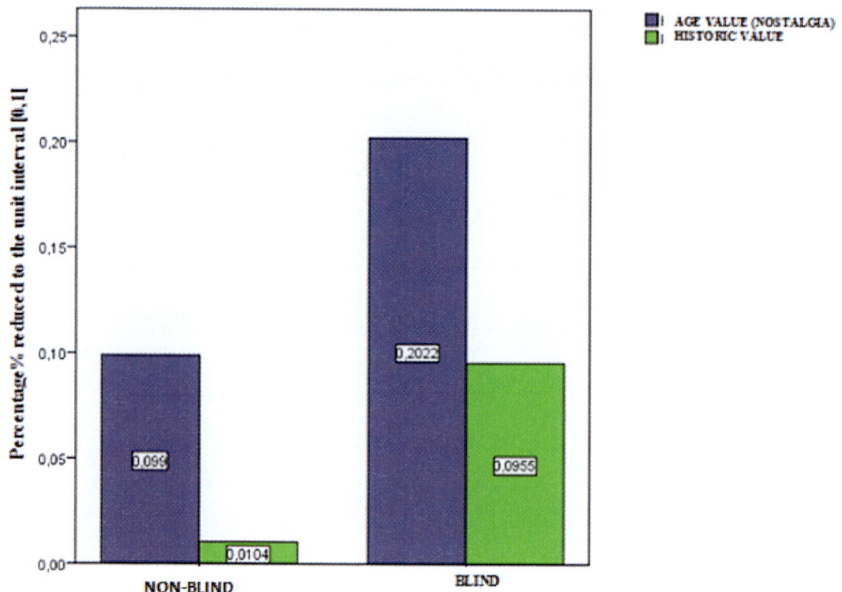

Diagram 6. Perception of monument values

Indeed, in Table 6, it is statistically confirmed that the age-value (nostalgia) that one may feel, as well as the historical value (recovery of information about the past) that one may recognise in certain landscape elements[2] hold the first position, mainly in the

---

[2] Examples of such reflections derived from the interviews are the following ones: "Rethimno (Crete-Greece) was an old-fashioned city, with labyrinth-curved stairs, vineyards, gardens, figs, beaches (1960–65), and now it looks like a miniature of

value system of the blind, and not so much in the value system of non-blind people. This could be interpreted as an attempt of the blind to reach the past, trying to exclude the visual reality of the present. In contrast, the attention of non-blind people centres mainly on the present. What they see is sufficient for them.

Table 6. Blindness and monument values

	BLINDNESS
AGE-VALUE	.150(**)
	.004
HISTORICAL VALUE	.193(**)
	.000

3.2 SENSES AND PERCEPTION OF LANDSCAPE ELEMENTS

Touching, as was presented in Table 2, is a basic monitoring sense of the blind. It does not focus on specific landscape features but has a broader usage. The blind seem to create a more focussed

---

Athens"; "Childhood (till 7 years old) in the village Elikona (Viotia-Greece), life in the village, despite poverty it was like a heaven in fir trees, fields, houses of stones, spending time with horse-riding, wood transport, seeds and threshing"; "Childhood in Kalamata (Peloponnesus-Greece) and since the age of 7 years in Athens. Everything outside of Athens was beautiful: mountain, the village Artemisia, there was only little traffic, rivers, camps in the village or at the sea"; "Till 20 years old in Chalkidiki, the river was appropriate for angling; I was moving stones, catching fishes, felt the platens and their shadows, the olive trees and the birds. The environment and the people there impressed me. We were cutting wood and constructing artifacts. I felt as an equal member with the others... years of deprivation, poverty"; "Three years in Lixouri (in Kefalonia), and Vlahada, 2 years in Athens. When the sun sets, it seems to sink in Ionian Sea – an opening at the edge of the sea, a stone that half of it moves to land and the other half to the sea. I remember the customs and traditions of Vlahada..."

impression of the landscape through their (imaginary) vision as well as sense of smell, exactly as the non-blind people do. They mainly see and smell landscape features, either imaginary or real ones. As noted previously (Diagram 2), the relatively increased (imaginary) visual perception can be attributed to the fact that in the research sample there were no born-blind people. This visual experience is focussed on the built environment and on the vegetation in general.

Smell relates to planting materials, particularly to the low vegetation. Despite the fact that in Diagram 4 and Table 4 the blindness does not seem to increase the perception of particular flora elements, in Table 7, which presents the role of senses, there is a slight tendency to perceive low vegetation through smell. This shows that what the blind people mean by "low vegetation" is not a grass "carpet" that ensures relaxation through smooth and unobstructed walking or a picnic, but mostly a mosaic of aromatic plants. In addition, despite the fact that in Diagram 4 the general perception of fauna by the blind is evident, none of the five senses concentrates on it, particularly in Table 7. So, the presence of animals becomes manifest through different senses.

Table 7. Mobilisation of senses in the blind group

	VISION	SMELL
BUILT	.274(**)	-.016
	.002	.855
VEGETATION	.286(**)	.237(**)
	.001	.007
LOW VEGETATION	.085	.227(**)
	.338	.010

As expected, in non-blind people, a broader spectrum of senses (all five of them) are stimulated and they perceive many more landscape features (Table 8). Vision is stimulated by the built environment, the flora (low and high plants, broad-leaved trees), and the fauna (especially mammals). Hearing seems to be atrophic in non-blind people' perceptions of landscape, in contrast to the findings of Carles et al. (1992). Smell seems to enhance the presence of plants in combination with vision. Taste is connected with the possibility of visiting built landscapes (e.g., tavern). Contrary to what would be expected, touching seems to play a more active role in non-blind individuals' landscapes than those of the blind, wherein it is absent. The non-blind people reinforce the presence of high and low vegetation and mammals by means of touching (e.g., soft grass, caressing of an animal).

Table 8. Mobilisation of senses in the non-blind group

	VISION	HEARING	SMELL	TASTE	TOUCH
STRUCTURED	.196(*)	.072	-.002	.204(*)	.006
	.015	.376	.983	.012	.945
VEGETATION	.283(**)	-.217(**)	.306(**)	-.018	.153
	.000	.007	.000	.821	.059
LOW VEGETATION	.238(**)	-.316(**)	.385(**)	.049	.204(*)
	.003	.000	.000	.550	.012
HIGH VEGETATION	.233(**)	-.178(*)	.223(**)	.094	.188(*)
	.004	.029	.006	.251	.021
BROAD-LEAVED TREES	.180(*)	-.153	.333(**)	-.074	.141
	.027	.062	.000	.370	.084
FAUNA	.201(*)	-.170(*)	-.124	-.082	.329(**)
	.013	.035	.126	.311	.000
MAMMALS	.164(*)	-.139	-.101	-.067	.337(**)
	.043	.088	.215	.411	.000

A landscape designer should take into consideration that, in contrast to non-blind people for whom all senses work together, in the blind not only is vision absent, but the general synergy among senses is restricted. In blind people, vision functions only in the imagination and can mostly recreate a built and green environment but not fauna. Their sense of smell focuses mainly on aromatic plants. Thus, designing a landscape for blind users can be made more effective if attention is given to the built environment and the low aromatic vegetation.

3.3 GENDER EFFECT

Gender influences the perception of landscape. As shown in Table 4, even if the blind in general do not pay more attention to fauna than the non-blind people do, in Table 9 there is a strong tendency on the part of blind women to perceive animal features more intensively than men and, in addition, there is a strong trend of nostalgia. According to the interview excerpts (e.g., "big parrot that talks, doggy"; "play, cajole, and talk with a cat"), blind women want to feel animals by their side, while men did not expressed such an interest. This can be attributed to the fact that these women had families and led more dynamic lives as compared to men who were bachelors, probably because of lack of self-confidence due to their blindness (e.g., "I don't get married by personal choice due to blindness"). Therefore, the way one experiences landscapes depends on the social relationships one has developed.

Table 9. Gender effect on the blind group

	MAN=1, WOMAN=2
FAUNA	.151(*)
	.033
NOSTALGIA	.250(**)
	.001

Because gender does not have a significant statistical effect on non-blind people, no table is placed here. Obviously, male or female non-blind people have equal opportunities of access to a landscape.

The landscape designer will probably get a greater response from female blind landscape users if he/she uses fauna features or elements of nostalgia such as the ones mentioned in section 3.1.6.

3.4 AGE EFFECT

As seen in Table 1, the blind do not present a greater need for symbols or indexes in order to create an alternative reality compared to non-blind people. This result is in accordance with the results of Table 10, where we see that the eldest avoid the involvement of indexes in the landscapes they perceive. In other words, ageing stands as a "filter" against complexity, since an index leads the observer to further landscape interpretations (e.g., Aristotle Square and "old town" in Thessaloniki).

As presented in Table 3, where blindness seems to "disdain" the aesthetics of architectural Functionalism, similarly as in Table 10, greater age in the blind seems to negatively affect the aesthetic dimension. This can be attributed to an extra difficulty in accessing landscapes due to age.

Table 10. Age effect on the blind group

	AGE
INDEX	-.131(*)
	.033
AESTHETICS	-.131(*)
	.044

In contrast to the blind, age in non-blind people does not induce any trend of disdain towards landscape or additional difficulty of access. On the contrary, it increases the importance of a landscape that is appropriate for strengthening social organisation (Table 11). Namely, it increases the importance of a landscape with the appropriate spatial structures that would enable the broadening of social networking ("friends in taverns, or somewhere else for drink or dance"; "parents' city, picturesque streets or places"; "friends going out for a coffee or a meal, companion going out for a coffee or a drink, or going to the beach").

Table 11. Age effect on the non-blind group

	AGE
SOCIAL ORGANISATION	.140(*)
	.022

Consequently, the designer of the landscape for the blind should take into account the previous discussion in sections 3.1.1 and 3.1.3 concerning the semiotic perception and the principles of Functionalism, especially when he/she designs landscapes for old blind people. A complex semiotic and aesthetic landscape conception should be avoided not because it would cause confusion for blind people but simply because it would not impress them. For instance, a garden with monuments or national plants would not be a strong attraction for the blind, especially the older ones. Moreover, social organisation is not an urgent need for older blind people but rather for non-blind people.

3.5 MARITAL STATUS EFFECT

In non-blind people, marital status presented no statistical correlation with any landscape variables. It was observed that married blind people have the tendency to ignore landscapes with traces (related to human action) (Table 12). This attitude can be attributed to their desire to relax from the monotonous or stressful reality induced by intense social relationships (Ulrich 1979; cf. Korpela and Ylen 2007; Wilson 2003). On the other hand, a single man would prefer a honeymoon in an intensely "civilized" environment (e.g., "Venice with gondolas" or "Eiffel Tower").

A critical question would be why no similar correlations appear among the non-blind people. A possible answer would be that the non-blind people can enjoy many pleasant features of the human environment to a much greater extent, or they would feel fed up with them. Thus, they do not tend to avoid it just because it is a monotonous or stressful landscape. Of course, this question remains open for future research.

Table 12. Marital status effect on the blind group

	SINGLE=0, MARRIED=1
TRACE	-.134(*)
	.029

The negative attitudes of married blind people towards anxiety and stress produced by the way of life and the environment of the cities may not be expressed directly through negativity towards the built environment, but it is expressed as negativity towards trace elements, which constitute a human intervention into space. If a designer wants to attract married blind people or blind people in general who want to escape from anxiety-inducing environments and monotony, he/she needs to use natural elements.

3.6 EDUCATION LEVEL EFFECT

Educated blind people tend to notice indexes and traces (Table 13). In particular, higher education appears to broaden the thinking and interests of the blind. Therefore, they perceive landscapes that include "access" (indexes) to an alternative, wider range of realities (e.g., fireplace → friends companionship; gondolas → honeymoon in Venice; Eiffel Tower → honeymoon in Paris). The high level of education seems to activate the interest of blind people for the human-made environment (trace) as well (e.g., "modern clubs with students"; "view from a balcony to a city"; "Rethimno in Crete, old city curving stairs – a miniature of Athens today"). Therefore, highly educated blind individuals present a tendency to be more interested in technical achievements that they are unable to see and do not try to escape from modern civilization. This is also in accordance with their positive attitude towards the built environment. In addition, their landscapes involve low vegetation that is compatible with the built environment, meaning that they like this harmonic combination of human-made and natural elements in a landscape. Moreover, in their everyday education activities, they feel the need for unimpeded and easy access to their destination, e.g., the place of their school or their urban environment in general, where they are dynamically trying to build a career.

Table 13. Effect of education level on the blind group

	UNIVERSITY GRADUATE (NO=0, YES=1)
INDEX	.218(**)
	.000
TRACE	.143(*)
	.020
BUILT ENVIRONMENT	.165(*)
	.020
LOW VEGETATION	.165(*)
	.020
TRANSPORT FACILITIES	.348(**)
	.000

In contrast to the blind, educated non-blind people do not have any particular transport or accessibility problems in accessing central urban areas. However, as far as built landscapes are concerned, there is a tendency for them to distance themselves from these because of the overstimulation that comes from viewing these and the massive amount of urbanism. The non-blind people regard urbanisation as a factor of oppression rather than as an admirable phenomenon.

Table 14. Effect of education level on the non-blind group

	UNIVERSITY GRADUATE (NO=0, YES=1)
TRANSPORT FACILITIES	-.162(**)
	.008
BUILT ENVIRONMENT	-.152(*)
	.024

The landscape architect who is expected to design an environment for blind students or degree-holders seeking a career should consider that blind people desire a landscape enriched with elements of a built environment (e.g., benches or elegant and elaborated architectural patterns) and at the same time is "balanced" with low vegetation and secure transport facilities, e.g., special corridors for the blind (Figure 2).

Figure 2. "Dutch system" for blind people at the campus of Aristotle University of Thessaloniki

3.7 EFFECT OF PLACE OF ORIGIN AND RESIDENCE

Although most principles of Functionalism do not attract the attention of blind people (Table 3), the place of origin and residence constitute two significant variables for the blinds' perception of landscape (Table 15). On the contrary, place of origin and residence have less of an effect on non-blind people (Table 16). The blind who were born, or are living, in urban areas pay attention to the landscape entertainment dimension and to the aesthetics. At the same time, they are sensitive to the ecological dimension of landscapes (e.g., "forest, snow, fireplace with

53

companionship, walking in the forest during the autumn or the summer, birds, grass, flowers, smells, sun, shadow") where the water element has a dominant presence.

Table 15. Effect of place of origin and residence on the blind group

	PLACE SIZE OF ORIGIN	PLACE SIZE OF RESIDENCE
ENTERTAINMENT	.136(*)	.205(**)
	.037	.002
AESTHETICS	.180(**)	.103
	.006	.115
ECOLOGY	.066	.202(**)
	.310	.002
WATER	.260(**)	.227(**)
	.000	.001

The non-blind people are not so sensitive to the peculiarities of their place of origin because of the landscape diversity they enjoy (e.g., from villages to cities). They have an amplitude of landscape scenes of aesthetic, ecological, and recreational importance. Thereby, they do not need to intensively unfold their imagination concerning their place of origin as blind people do. Only the geomorphologic features and the water element (e.g., "sea, land, sunset at the beach") make an emotional impact on the non-blind people of urban areas.

Table 16. Effect of place of origin and residence on the non-blind group

	PLACE OF ORIGIN	RESIDENCE
GEOMORPHOLOGY	.098	.132(*)
	.144	.049
WATER	.220(**)	.082
	.001	.227

It is understandable that a designer who intends to create a landscape for the blind with intense imagery of big urban places should take into consideration their need for entertainment, ecology, and aesthetics especially. The aesthetic dimension, even if it is abstract, can be framed as "landscape diversity", such as urban open areas with appropriate vegetation that may have an impact on the micro-climate, with grass, pebbles, or stones, along with the right sound environment (plant fences that will minimise urban noises, tranquil music), water, "technical smart constructions" like little bridges for combating spatial monotony, even in places where there is no water (Stavridis 1990). Water seems to emotionally move blind people in big urban areas as much as non-blind people. It is, thus, a design option with broad acceptance.

3.8 EFFECT OF SOCIAL CLASS ON BLIND PEOPLE

Feelings regarding social class were measured only in the blind group, since all non-blind interviewees considered themselves to belong to the middle class and there was no variability. A two-step cluster analysis was conducted. We present only the clusters in which the social classes present significant variability (Bonferroni test).

a) Social class and semiotic perception

The clusters where the social class (low, middle, or upper) seems to be significantly related with the semiotic landscape variables are presented in Table 17:

Table 17. Social class and semiotic perception in the blind group

Two-Step Cluster analysis	Clusters (concise presentation)		
Variables	1	2	3
Social class	0: low 59: middle 0: upper	17: low 0: middle 34: upper	0: low 62: middle 0: upper
Icon	59	51	62
Index	0	0	2
Symbol	0	1	0
Trace	0	28	62
Metaphor	0	0	0

It is observed that middle class blind people tend to perceive icons (cluster 1) or icons combined with traces (cluster 3). The lower and upper classes are also characterised by their perceptions of icons and traces (cluster 2). The semiotic variables that seem to be irrelevant to the social class are the most complex ones (index, symbol, metaphor). Thus, one can assume that they depend more on internal factors (e.g., personal experiences, idiosyncrasy) and not on one's social position.

b) Social class and landscape elements

In Table 18, we observe that upper class blind people tend to perceive built landscape elements (cluster 2). This can be attributed to the fact that they come from urban areas. There are very few cases of blind people from both the lower and upper classes (cluster 3) who appear to be attracted by the flora. The middle class does not show any differentiation in perceiving built landscapes or flora elements (cluster 1 and cluster 4).

Table 18. Social class and landscape elements in the blind group

Two-Step Cluster analysis	Clusters (concise presentation)			
Variables	1	2	3	4
Social classes	0: low 45: middle 0: upper	0: low 0: middle 19: upper	5: low 0: middle 8: upper	0: low 35: middle 0: upper
Built environment	45	19	0	35
Flora	0	5	5	35

Concerning the semiotic perception, a designer who is going to design a landscape for blind people can take into account that all classes prefer the simplest possible approach (perception of icons or traces). There is no point in trying to create broad appeal through complex semiotics. The semiotic perception is mainly a personal matter, and one should not lose time trying to find symbols and indexes that are supposed to attract a particular class.

More useful information for class-specific design concerns the perception of landscape elements. From clusters A and B, it is evident that the designer can turn the attention of the middle and upper classes to elements of the built environment. At the same time, he/she can use plants as a possible tool for bridging the lower and upper classes.

3.9 LANDSCAPE TYPOLOGY

3.9.1 SENSES COMBINATION

In Table 19, it is observed that in blind people's landscapes, visual and hearing elements function competitively and not complementarily. It is obvious that hearing replaces vision. For instance, when they imagine a river that flows, they do not necessarily feel the need to hear its sound, or when they actually visit a river, they do not have to visualise it in their imaginations. The blind seem to feel the need to choose among audio and visual features while perceiving the landscape they are imagining or experiencing. On the other hand, the visual imagination seems to complete and not to compete with the sense of smell. In other words, they feel the need to visualise the smell of a landscape so as to give value to it (for instance, they associate the smell from the Easter lamb with the family gathering during Easter holidays). In contrast to smell, taste also seems to capture their attention really strongly and to exclude vision as an unnecessary factor. Hearing competes with taste. Additionally, it is observed that not only vision but also touching replaces hearing. Touching the landscape seems to constitute an autonomous value, since it does not have a significant positive correlation with any other sense. Thus, the significance of touching in order to confirm reality is clear. This result supports also the data of Table 2.

It is also remarkable that smell and taste are statistically independent. Finally, taste seems to compete with touching. This leads to the autonomous value of both of those senses (taste and touch landscape).

Table 19. Interaction of the senses in the blind group

	Hearing	Smell	Taste	Touch
Vision (imaginary)	-.354(**)	.170(*)	-.212(**)	-.113
	.000	.025	.005	.139
Hearing		.000	-.160(*)	-.276(**)
		1.000	.035	.000
Smell			-.053	.007
			.484	.930
Taste				-.149(*)
				.050

The combination of the senses in the blind does not differ from the combination in non-blind people, as seen in the Table 20. An important factor for this similarity might be that the interviews were conducted in blind people who were not blind from birth and that they had experience the world of non-blind people.

Table 20. Interaction of the senses in the non-blind group

	Hearing	Smell	Taste	Touch
Vision	-.535(**)	.206(**)	-.263(**)	.017
	.000	.003	.000	.813
Hearing		-.121	-.161(*)	-.274(**)
		.086	.022	.000
Smell			-.035	.128
			.625	.070
Taste				-.096
				.175

Apart from the visual landscape, which the landscape designer designs for the non-blind people, he/she can also create four other landscapes that will be suitable for blind people: hearing, smell, taste, and touch landscapes. From the combinations mentioned above, the designer should be aware of the following ones: he/she can help the blind to visualise landscapes through smell (aromatic flowers, artificial sea odours, artificial or real food odours that remind one of special occasions and landscapes such as anniversaries). Three of the four landscapes (touch, sound, and taste landscapes) seem to be independent from the need to visualise. Touching can be flexibly used for creating innovative situations and fighting monotony thanks to its autonomy (e.g., benches made of various materials other than ordinary wood, such as bronze). Taste and hearing can also be used by the designer autonomously. Especially hearing can be used for the creation of "soundscapes", e.g., zones with animal sounds, urban sounds, music, etc. Interchanging these zones can remove monotony. In addition, the appropriate creation of sounds (e.g, walking on pebbles) can trigger feelings of age-value (nostalgia) or historical value (information about the past), for instance in a park, since it reminds one of older forms of road construction. Another example is the sound of a fountain that can prompt the recall of sounds of the modern era. Similarly, the sound of walking on gravel may lead to a feeling of care and affection (Hedfors and Berg 2003).

3.9.2 COMBINATION OF LANDSCAPE ELEMENTS

In Table 21 it can be seen that there is no antagonistic relationship between flora and the built environment. Such a relationship exists between built environments and fauna as well as between built environments and the geomorphology. However, despite this "devastating" character of the built environment, this appears to be compatible with water elements and imaginary representations of air- and sky-related environments. Nothing impedes the existence of fountains in a stone-built square or the enjoyment of the sky's view in a city.

The plant elements and in particular the low vegetation is quite compatible for the fauna and especially the birds. However, the blind do not seem to be willing to associate a landscape with intensive geomorphologic features with rich flora elements. Plants actually compete with geomorphology in blind people's perception of landscapes. Water and air- and sky-related elements, as previously mentioned, are compatible with flora and built environments.

Fauna landscape elements comprise mammals, and especially birds. However, fauna is supplanted by geomorphology. Even if geomorphology seems to monopolise the observer's attention – as it appears to be competitive with the aforementioned elements – it relates positively with water (e.g., "beach, island", etc). A similar relationship is observed between water and air-sky element (e.g. "when the sun sets it seems to sink into the Ionian Sea").

Table 21. Correlations of elements of landscape for the blind group

	FLORA	FAUNA	MAMMALS	BIRDS	GEOMOR-PHOLOGY	WATER	AIR-SKY
BUILT ENVIRONMENT	-.082	.201(**)	-.268(**)	-.106	-.265(**)	.014	-.007
	.252	.004	.000	.135	.000	.849	.920
FLORA		.188(**)	-.041	.154(*)	-.153(*)	.133	-.111
		.008	.568	.030	.031	.061	.118
LOW VEGETATION		.176(*)	-.017	.281(**)	-.043	-.043	-.009
		.013	.810	.000	.548	.543	.902
FAUNA			.598(**)	.626(**)	-.146(*)	.046	-.050
			.000	.000	.040	.523	.483
BIRDS					-.153(*)	.083	-.031
					.031	.245	.660
GEOMORPHOLOGY						.195(**)	.112
						.006	.115
WATER							.203(**)
							.004

In contrast to the blind, the non-blind individuals' perceptions of landscape present a more complex typology (Table 22). The non-blind people are not indifferent towards the vegetation type that appears in a built landscape. They are used to imagining it with high vegetation, broad-leaved trees, and fruit-bearing plants (e.g., olive tree). Moreover, the non-blind people maintain a closer relationship with everyday spatial reality and thereby they can not imagine a landscape where cement dominates combined with water and air-sky elements, or with mammals and elaborated geomorphology (Maruani and Amit-Cohen 2007). Thus, blindness partly creates a tendency of embellishing the reality.

Moreover, in contrast to the blind, who are indifferent towards the vegetation types, in the non-blind individuals' perceptions of landscape, there is an extensive range of differentiated and inter-complementary flora elements. The non-blind people desire a combination of all type of vegetation: low, high, decorative and aromatic, coniferous and broad-leaved plants and fruit-bearing plants.

The non-blind people associate low vegetation with birds, as do blind people. At the same time, they also associate high vegetation with birds, in contrast to the blind. Furthermore, non-blind people prefer low vegetation without mammals, while the blind have no such preference. Vegetation is incompatible with the perception of geomorphologic features as well.

Aromatic plants are associated with the air-sky elements and conifers are associated with water. Such correlations do not exist in landscapes as perceived by the blind.

As far as fauna is concerned, non-blind people prefer mammals over birds; the reverse of what is true for the blind group. There is no room for fauna, and especially mammals, in a landscape with intensive geomorphologic and water elements. This is another aspect of differentiation from landscapes of the blind. As with the blind, geomorphologic features can be combined with water, and water with air-sky elements.

Table 22. Correlations of elements of landscape for the non-blind group

	FLORA	LOW VEGETATION	HIGH VEGETATION	DECORATIVE PLANTS	AROMATIC PLANTS	CONIFEROUS	BROAD-LEAVED	FRUIT-BEARING PLANTS	FAUNA	MAMMALS	BIRDS	GEOMORPHOLOGY	WATER	AIR-SKY
BUILT ENVIRONMENT	.118	.096	.173(*)	.094	-.068	.131	.185(**)	.137(*)	-.094	-.183(**)	.047	-.332(**)	-.192(**)	-.250(**)
	.080	.156	.010	.165	.314	.053	.006	.042	.161	.006	.483	.000	.004	.000
FLORA		.737(**)	.678(**)	.316(**)	.345(**)	.187(**)	.372(**)	.267(**)	.011	-.104	.110	-.172(*)	-.015	.033
		.000	.000	.000	.000	.005	.000	.000	.871	.123	.104	.010	.820	.628
LOW VEGETATION			.480(**)	.328(**)	.468(**)	.090	.333(**)	.246(**)	-.009	-.135(*)	.178(**)	-.151(*)	-.049	.112
			.000	.000	.000	.182	.000	.000	.894	.046	.008	.025	.469	.098
HIGH VEGETATION				.308(**)	.168(*)	.276(**)	.458(**)	.394(**)	.052	-.124	.199(**)	-.143(*)	-.028	-.118
				.000	.013	.000	.000	.000	.439	.067	.003	.034	.682	.080
DECORATIVE PLANTS					.296(**)	.281(**)	.600(**)	.290(**)	-.071	-.058	-.039	-.139(*)	-.072	-.055
					.000	.000	.000	.000	.298	.395	.570	.040	.289	.416
AROMATIC PLANTS						-.034	.391(**)	.466(**)	-.077	-.063	-.042	.022	.039	.364(**)
						.613	.000	.000	.254	.351	.534	.750	.669	.000
CONIFEROUS							.503(**)	-.027	-.042	-.034	-.023	-.083	.195(**)	-.033
							.000	.696	.536	.613	.736	.222	.004	.629
BROAD-LEAVED								.718(**)	-.019	-.068	-.046	-.083	-.034	-.065
								.000	.776	.314	.502	.220	.615	.336
FRUIT-BEARING PLANTS									.027	-.049	-.033	-.008	-.136(*)	-.047
									.693	.471	.631	.906	.044	.491
FAUNA										.815(**)	.545(**)	-.186(**)	-.147(*)	-.073
										.000	.000	.005	.029	.278
MAMMALS											.076	-.153(*)	-.177(**)	-.060
											.259	.023	.009	.375
BIRDS														
GEOMORPHOLOGY													-.328(**)	.034
													.000	.615
WATER														.171(*)
														.011

In general, the landscape designer should take into consideration that his/her duty is simpler in designing landscapes for the blind, even if their worlds could be characterised as more complex because of the different ways of perceiving things. It is not necessary to examine in detail the types of vegetation designers incorporate into the design. The blind are more willing to accept a combination of built environments and water, or of fauna and water, than are non-blind people. The designer should be aware of blind people's preferences for birds over mammals, in contrast to non-blind people, who prefer the opposite. Therefore, the designer can be more flexible when structuring a landscape for blind users.

3.9.3 COMBINATION OF FUNCTIONALISM PRINCIPLES

Table 23 shows that blind people tend to connect socialising with place of residence and to separate it from entertainment. This illustrates loneliness. The development of social contacts is directly connected with the chances for social networking (making acquaintances) the place offers. It is characteristic that they do not relate socialising to the ecologic dimension (e.g., parks). Finally, they do not feel that socialisation is dependent on transport possibilities.

The need to work seems to be related only to transport. In landscapes for the blind, places of residence and entertainment do not appear together. However, the need for combining residences and social networking places is evident (e.g., "I know by descriptions that in Kozani there is a landscape with pine trees, lakes, springs, rivers, and a big square in the centre of the city – twice as large as the square in Kalamata – cafeterias, shops, and trees around; in general, it is a clean city"). Entertainment is associated with the ecological dimensions of the place, whereas it seems to be rather incompatible with social networking (e.g., "overcrowded cafeterias"). The aesthetic dimension is connected with the ecological one. Nevertheless, the ecological dimension is incompatible with social organisation as well as with transport, as long as they are based on human-made environments.

Table 23. Correlations of Functionalism principles in landscapes for the blind group

	RESIDENCE	ENTERTAINMENT	ECOLOGY	SOCIAL ORGANISATION (NETWORKING)	POSSIBILITY OF TRANSPORT
SOCIALISATION	.260(*)	-.307(**)	-.150	.589(**)	.149
	.016	.004	.169	.000	.432
WORK	.109	-.058	-.033	.097	.344(**)
	.095	.375	.616	.140	.000
RESIDENCE		-.239(**)	-.102	.310(**)	.098
		.000	.118	.000	.267
ENTERTAINMENT			.412(**)	-.270(**)	-.062
			.000	.000	.481
AESTHETICS			.432(**)	-.090	-.113
			.000	.170	.199
ECOLOGY				-.214(**)	-.246(**)
				.001	.005

Similar to the combination of landscape elements, in spatial functions the non-blind people have a desire for more complexity (more correlations in Table 24). For non-blind people, socialisation elements in landscapes seems to replace the need for aesthetics and to be strongly and positively correlated with ecology. The aspect of work does not appear together with entertainment, aesthetics, and ecology in the same landscape, while in the landscapes for the blind, work is not considered to be incompatible with these three functions. Similar issues concerning residence are present when looking at how the blind perceive landscapes. Entertainment appears to be viewed positively regarding its relation to ecology, as with the blind's perception of landscapes, but it is not correlated with social organisation. Aesthetics are also positively correlated with ecology. Here, social organisation is directly connected to transport due to the intense mobility of non-blind people.

Table 24. Correlations of Functionalism principles in landscapes for the non-blind group

	RESIDENCE	ENTERTAINMENT	AESTHETICS	ECO-LOGY	SOCIAL ORGANISATION	POSSIBILITY OF TRANSPORT
SOCIALISATION	.339(**)	-.272(*)	-.261(*)	.446(**)	.692(**)	.139
	.004	.023	.029	.000	.000	.252
WORK	.010	-.185(**)	-.192(**)	-.138(*)	.069	.074
	.867	.002	.002	.025	.262	.229
RESIDENCE		-.247(**)	.061	-.068	.266(**)	.159(**)
		.000	.319	.267	.000	.009
ENTERTAINMENT			-.032	.356(**)	.037	.044
			.605	.000	.550	.473
AESTHETICS				.328(**)	.086	.039
				.000	.161	.521
SOCIAL ORGANISATION						.214(**)
						.000

Useful information for the landscape designer is that in landscapes for the blind, socialisation is not significantly in contrast to the aesthetic function and is independent from the ecological dimension, in contrast to landscapes for non-blind people. In the blind's perception of landscapes, the work environment is not incompatible with aesthetics, entertainment, and ecology, in contrast to the non-blind people. Moreover, for the blind, entertainment is incompatible with social networking, contrary to non-blind people. Thus, designers should be more flexible in designing landscapes for the blind regarding Functionalism principles, apart from the case of entertainment, which seems to require a not overcrowded environment.

4 CONCLUSIONS, SUGGESTIONS, AND LIMITATIONS

4.1 CONCLUSIONS

- Semiotic perception

The landscape that is perceived both by non-blind people and the blind is characterised by a similar semiotic structure. An overwhelming amount is composed of icons, and to a limited extent indexes or symbols and metaphors.

- Use of senses

The role of the senses in the perception of landscapes is quite similar in the blind and in non-blind people. Vision plays a dominant role in both groups (in the blind it is realised as imaginary vision). Second comes touching, while in third place comes hearing. Last come taste and smell.

- Principles of Functionalism

The need for socialisation plays a primary role in the landscapes of non-blind people and the blind. Another significant landscape aspect for both groups is the ecological dimension. The aspect of residence especially seems to be more important for the blind interviewees because they do not move about as much as non-blind people.

- Built and natural environments

For the blind, the flora in landscapes appear with an abstract character. The blind are not very demanding about the shape of flora. To a more restricted degree, fauna, and especially mammals and birds, also appear. An appropriately built environment can become a necessity for the blind, while a flora environment continues to be significant but a secondary priority. The reverse is observed for the non-blind people.

- Perception of the landscape's physical condition

In the blind, geomorphology and water do make an impact, while the blind's attention to air- and sky-related elements (e.g., clouds and sunset), even imaginary ones, is not really intense.

Water and the geomorphologic structure seem to be of importance for the landscape of both groups, since they stimulate the sense of touch, too.

- Perception of monument values

Nostalgia and historical value play a weak role in landscapes for non-blind people since the present largely monopolises their attention. On the contrary, the blind seem to live mainly with their memories. This can be explained by the blind's tendency to escape into the past, which is an attempt to outbalance the inaccessibility to the visual reality in the present.

- Senses and perception of landscape elements

The blind seem to create the impression called "landscape" mainly through their (imaginary) vision as well as through smell, as non-blind people do. What they do is to see and smell landscape elements, either real or imaginary. Smell seems to focus on flora elements, and on low vegetation in particular.

- Gender effect

In blind women, one can observe a stronger tendency to perceive fauna features than in blind men, as well as a special tendency for nostalgia. In non-blind people, gender did not present any statistically significant effects.

- Age effect

Older people avoid acknowledging indexes in landscapes they perceive. They also seem to disregard the aesthetic dimension. This can be attributed to the difficulties in accessing landscapes due to age-induced problems. In addition, social organisation does not seem to be an urgent need for old blind people. This is not true in the case of the non-blind people.

- Marital status effect

Married blind people are usually indifferent to landscapes with traces of human action. This can be attributed to their desire for relaxation from the monotony or anxiety of intense social relations.

- Education level effect

The blind with high education levels desire to perceive landscapes that include "passages" (indexes) to an alternative, wider range of realities. They are interested in human action features (traces) that they can not see, and they do not express a tendency to escape from modern civilization, in contrast to non-blind people. They opt for low vegetation and they feel an urgent need for easy, comfortable transport and free access.

- Effect of place of origin and residence

The blind that come from urban areas or live there seem to give special attention to the entertainment dimension of the landscape and to the aesthetic value, too. At the same time, a special preference is shown for the ecological dimensions of the landscape when water is distinctly present. The non-blind people are less stimulated by the particularities of their places of origin or residence due to their numerousness.

- The effects of social class

Blind people of all social classes seem to perceive icons or traces, while the perception of more complex signs (index, symbol, metaphor) is not correlated with the social class. Individuals who feel they belong to high social classes perceive built elements. There is also a slight tendency in the lower and higher class to be more familiar with the flora.

- Combination of senses

In the landscapes of blind people, the visual and sound elements compete with each other. The visual imagination seems to complement smell, while taste seems to attract their attention more strongly and to exclude vision as an unnecessary landscape dimension. The touch landscape apparently constitutes an autonomous value. The combination of senses in people who are not blind from birth is similar to that in non-blind people.

- Combination of landscape elements

For the blind, there seems to be no incompatibility between flora and built environments in a landscape. Antagonistic relationships appear between built environments and fauna as well as between built environments and geomorphologic features. Also, built environments appear to be compatible with water, in contrast to the non-blind people. Blind people are more susceptible to the combination of fauna and water than non-blind people.

Contrary to the blind, the non-blind individuals' landscapes are characterised by a more complex and demanding typology. The non-blind people are not indifferent to the flora types that appear in a built landscape. Furthermore, the non-blind people can hardly imagine a built environment combined with water elements. Both the blind and non-blind people associate low vegetation with birds. Concerning fauna, the non-blind people mainly opt for mammals rather than birds, in contrast to the blind.

- Combinations of Functionalism principles

The blind tend to vigorously connect socialising to place of residence and to separate it from entertainment. This is evidence of loneliness. The need for a job is associated only with transport. Entertainment is associated with the ecological dimension of space, while it seems to be rather incompatible with the social networking capacity of a place. The aesthetic dimension is associated with the ecological one. In non-blind people, work does not appear together with entertainment, aesthetics, and ecological values in the same landscape, while in landscapes of the blind, work is not considered incompatible with these three elements.

4.2 SUGGESTIONS FOR DESIGNING

- As far as the use of senses is concerned:

It is important for the designer to know that, apart from the visual landscape of non-blind people, there are four more landscapes that may stimulate the blind: hearing, smell, taste, and touch. The blind have the chance to visualise landscape through smell. The remaining three landscapes are independent from the need to visualising. Especially touch can be flexibly used to ward against monotony. Taste and hearing can also be used in an autonomous way. Especially hearing can be used for the creation of "soundscapes".

Designers should take into consideration that sight can be activated continually in a blind person's imagination.

Designers can use auxiliary elements for structuring a landscape, such as music, smells, and tastes, that remind the blind of the past.

It would also be advisable to take into account that, in contrast to non-blind people where there is a synergy between all senses, in the blind, not only sight is absent, but the synergy between senses is also quite weak. Most senses function diffusedly in the environment. In the blind, mainly (imaginary) sight can reconstruct built environments and flora, and smell is mainly focussed on aromatic plants. Thus, a landscape design for the blind could be more effective if extra attention is paid to built environments and to aromatic low vegetation.

- As far as semiotics is concerned:

From a semiotic point of view, a simple design is advisable for the blind as well as for non-blind people. It is recommendable for the designer of landscapes for the blind to avoid complex landscape conceptions, not because it would confuse the blind but because it does not touch them emotionally.

- As far as Functionalism is concerned:

In order to set acceptable priorities for the blind, the designer should know that in landscapes for non-blind people, the need for entertainment and aesthetics is demanding due to the need for socialisation, whereas in landscapes for blind persons, these dimensions are secondary (aesthetics, entertainment, work, etc.). The primary need for blind people in a landscape is socialisation.

In addition, it would be advisable to take into consideration that the work environment is not incompatible with aesthetics, entertainment, and ecological values in landscapes for the blind. On the contrary, in non-blind people, work seems to be by definition an aspect that they try to eliminate and to isolate from the other aspects of their lives. In general, a designer has more flexibility in creating a landscape for the blind in terms of Functionalism, apart from the case of entertainment, which seems to be incompatible with overcrowded environments.

In the case of the blind who have vivid representations of urban centres, either because of their residence or because of their origins, the designer should involve special planning for entertainment, ecological expectations, and aesthetics. The aesthetic dimension can be specified for the blind as landscape diversity. Water seems to be a solution with broad acceptance both for the blind and non-blind people.

- As far as the landscape synthesis is concerned:

The role of a landscape designer seems to be simpler when he/she designs a landscape for the blind, since it is not necessary to take caution with the types of vegetation, and also since the blind have more positive attitudes towards the combination of built environments and water elements than non-blind people. They are also more positive towards a combination of water and fauna elements. Another suggestion for the designer is to take into account the preferences of the blind for birds over mammals, which is in contrast to the non-blind people.

A designer may use as a criterion the fact that both built environments and flora play dominant roles in the landscapes perceived by the blind and also the non-blind people. In designing landscapes for the blind, emphasis should be given to the existence of fauna.

It is also important that he/she knows that while non-blind people can be impressed with water elements, this is not the case for the blind, where a balanced use of geomorphologic shaping and water elements is indispensable.

- As far as the social characteristics of the blind landscape users are concerned:

If a designer wants to attract married blind visitors or blind visitors who want to escape from anxiety or monotony, then he/she should use natural elements. As shown, this is not necessarily true for non-blind people.

A designer can create a stronger resonance in female landscape users if he/she uses fauna and age-value (nostalgia) elements.

If a designer is going to design an environment for blind students or graduates who are after a career, then he/she should bear in mind that this group would be interested in a landscape enriched with built elements and low vegetation as well as with secure facilities of transport.

It is also advisable to remember that all social classes prefer the simplest possible approach (icon and trace). The semiotic perception is a personal matter. A designer can easily turn the attention of the middle and upper classes to elements of built environments and use flora as a possible medium of bringing the middle and upper classes closer.

4.3 LIMITATIONS AND QUESTIONS FOR FUTURE RESEARCH

As with every empirical research project, this one is characterised by certain limitations that are stated below so as to become grounds for future research.

- *Points of improvement in the Methodology*

The sample of blind people in this particular work is restricted to people who are not blind from birth. Thus, the question is whether people who are blind from birth would exhibit the same features (e.g., in the combination of the senses or the perception of

Functionalism principles). A broader future sample could be gathered in the future (this could also include children).

A juxtaposition between the blind's social class consciousness and that of non-blind people was not feasible because non-blind people were characterised by the same class consciousness. This could be a challenge for future researchers.

Another point for future researchers to consider is that a bivariate analysis was conducted, since this work is just a primary exploration of a relatively unknown scientific field. A cluster analysis has been applied only regarding social class. In the future, a cluster analysis is likely to take place across a wider range of variables. Multivariate Analysis or Principal Component Analysis regarding social and landscape variables can be employed in order to extract a more detailed typology, if an adequate variability is achieved.

The specific research was quite time-consuming because it was based on semi-structured interviews and was characterised by a quite intensive qualitative part. The text of the interviews should be analysed quantitatively in order to produce statistical correlations. For future research, a standardised questionnaire can be formulated on the basis of the results of this research in order to verify these results and to produce further conclusions.

- *Points for improvement in Theorising*

Although it was attempted to understand the differences in perception between non-blind people and the blind on the basis of the interviews, several points still leave open questions for further research (e.g., why married blind people hold a different attitude towards human-made landscapes than married non-blind people).

This research, as a primary one, remains at a strategic planning level. This was also its initial objective (general explorations and suggestions to designers). Future research based on the present results can progress to a more detailed analysis and propose alternative specific illustrative solutions for landscape design (e.g., parks, schools playgrounds).

SUMMARY

The aim of this research is to explore how the blind perceive the landscape in comparison with non-blind people and to provide suggestions to landscape designers. The research is based on interviews and statistical analysis. A classical assumption in Landscape Sociology and the Anthropology of Senses is that there exists not only a visual landscape but landscapes that are constructed by the remaining four senses (hearing, smell, touch, and taste) and that landscape is a subjective impression created by a place. The blind's perception of landscape was examined from various points of view (Semiotics, Functionalism, perception of landscape elements and monument values).

The main findings were that the workplace is not incompatible with aesthetic, entertainment, and ecological values in the blind's perception of landscape, in contrast to non-blind people. In addition, blind students or graduates are interested in a landscape enriched with built elements, low vegetation, and transport facilities. In the case of the blind who have intensive experiences of big urban areas due to their residence or origins, a special care should be taken for needs of entertainment, ecological values, and aesthetics. The aesthetic dimension can be specified for the blind as landscape diversity. Water elements seem to constitute a solution of broad acceptance both for the blind and non-blind people. A designer should know that even if he/she could easily impress non-blind people by means of water elements, this is not necessarily true in the case of the blind landscape users, for whom a balanced use of geomorphologic shaping with water elements seems to be essential.

REFERENCES

Literature:

Ananiadou-Tzimopoulou, M. (1992) *Landscape Architecture. Design of urban places. Critical approach and theory, contemporary tendencies in landscape design* (orig. Greek) Vol. A. Publ. Ziti. Thessaloniki.

Bolou, M. and Gkouveris, V. (2000) *New horizons for kids with vision problems. Guide of immediate action* (orig. Greek). Thessaloniki. Publ. Iera Mitropolis of Thessaloniki.

Botton, A.N. (2008) *Architecture of happiness* (orig. Greek). Publ. Pataki. Athens.

Chen, C.-H., Chang, W.-C. and Chang, W.-T. (2008) Gender differences in relation to wayfinding strategies, navigational support design, and wayfinding task difficulty. *Journal of Environmental Psychology* 29(2): 220-226.

Coluccia, E., Losue, G. and Brandimonte, M. A. (2007) The relationship between map drawing and spatial orientation abilities: A study of gender differences. *Journal of Environmental Psychology* 27(2): 135–144.

Crooks, V.A., Dorn, M.L. and Wilton, R. D. (2008) Emerging scholarship in the geographies of disability. *Health & Place* 14(4): 883-888.

Dimen, L. and Palamariu, M. (2007) Environment & Landscape- A computing approach. (Edit.) N. Eleftheriadis, A. Styliadis, I. Paliokas. *Proceedings of the International Conference LANT07. Landscape Architecture and New Technologies.* Pp. 129-141. Department of Landscape Architecture. Technological Educational Institute of Kavala. Drama- Greece.

Doevendans, K., Lörzing, H. and Schram, A. (2007) From modernist landscapes to New Nature: Planning of rural utopias in the Netherlands. *Landscape Research* 32(3): 333-354.

Dzitac I., S.M. and Valeanu, E.M. (2007) Web Distributed Computing for Landscape Architecture. (Edit.) N. Eleftheriadis, A. Styliadis, I.Paliokas. *Proceedings of the International Conference. LANT07. Landscape Architecture and New Technologies.* Pp. 25-35. Department of Landscape Architecture. Technological Educational Institute of Kavala. Drama- Greece.

Eleftheriadis, N. (2008) *Landscape management* (orig. Greek). Drama. Publ. Charis.

Espinosa, M. A., Ungar, S., Ochaíta, E., Blades, M. and Spencer, C. (1998) Comparing methods for introducing blind and visually impairing people to unfamiliar urban environments. *Journal of Environmental Psychology* 18(3): 277-287.

Hedfors, P. and Berg, P. G. (2003) The sounds of two landscape settings: Auditory concepts for physical planning and design. *Landscape Research* 28(3): 245–263.

Carles, J., Bernáldez, F. and Lucio, J.d. (1992) Audio-visual interactions and soundscape preferences. *Landscape Research* 17(2): 52–56.

Hall, E. and Kearns, R. (2001) Making space for the "intellectual" in geographies of disability. *Health & Place* 7(3): 237–246.

Hasanagas, N. (2004) *Power factor typology through organizational and network analysis. Using environmental policy networks as an illustration.* Publ. Ibidem. Stuttgart.

Hasanagas, N.D. (2010) *Landscape sociology* (orig. Greek). Publ. Papasotiriou. Athens.

Hasanagas, N.D., Styliadis, A.D., Papadopoulou, E.I., and Birtsas, P.K. (2010). Land Policy & Socio-Spatial Impacts in a burned forest: The case of Chalkidiki, Greece (2006). *RevCAD – Journal of Geodesy and Cadastre (forthcoming)*.

Hoeppner, C., Frick, J. and Buchecker, M. (2008) What drives people's willingness to discuss local landscape development? *Landscape Research* 33(5): 605–622.

Herrington, S. and Lesmeister, C. (2006) The design of landscapes at child-care centres: Seven Cs. *Landscape Research* 31(1): 63–82.

Holt, L. (2003) (Dis)abling children in primary school microspaces: Geographies of inclusion and exclusion. *Health & Place* 9(2): 119–128.

Jones, M. (2007) The European landscape convention and the question of public participation. *Landscape Research* 32(5): 613–633.

Kim, M.-H., Cho, T.-B. and Kim, K.-H. (2008) Residents' attitudes to landscape and ecology of idyllic housing sites: The case of South Korea. *Landscape Research* 33(4): 487–501.

Korpela, K. M. and Ylén, M. (2007) Perceived health is associated with visiting natural favourite places in the vicinity. *Health & Place* 13(1): 138–151.

Lawson, B. (2003) *The language of space*. Publ. Elsevier. Oxford.

Maruani, T. and Amit-Cohen, I. (2007) Open-space planning models: A review of approaches and methods. *Landscape and Urban Planning* 81(1–2): 1–13.

Meining, D. W. (1979) The beholding eye: Ten versions of the same scene. D.W. Meining (Edit.) *The interpretation of ordinary landscapes: Geographical Essays.* Pp. 33–48. Oxford University Press. New York.

Moore-Colyer, R. and Scott, A. (2005) What kind of landscape do we want? Past, present and future perspectives. *Landscape Research* 30(4): 501–523.

Nikolaidou, S. (1993) *Social organization of urban places* (orig. Greek). Publ. Papazisi. Athens.

Ode, A., Tveit, M.S. and Fry, G. (2008) Capturing landscape visual character using indicators: Touching base with landscape aesthetic theory. *Landscape Research* 33(1): 89–117.

O'Rourke, E. (2005) Landscape planning and community participation: Local lessons from Mullaghmore, the Burren National Park, Ireland. *Landscape Research* 30(4): 483–500.

Ottosson, J. and Grahn, P. (2005) A comparison of leisure time spent in a garden with leisure time spent indoors: On measures of restoration in residents in geriatric care. *Landscape Research* 30(1): 23–55.

Palmer, C. and Brady, E. (2007) Landscape and value in the work of Alfred Wainwright (1907–1991). *Landscape Research* 32(4): 397–421.

Panopoulos, P. (2005) Ethnographic and historical approaches of the Sound. P. Panopoulos (Edit.) *From the music to the Sound* (orig. Greek). Pp. 217–242. Publ. Alexandria. Athens.

Riegl, A. (1982) The modern cult of monuments. Its character and its origin [1903]. *Oppositions* 25: 21–51.

Read, M. (2005) Planning and the picturesque: A case study of the Dunedin District Plan and its application to the management of the landscape of the Otago Peninsula. *Landscape Research* 30(3): 337–359.

Smardon, R.C. (1988) Perception and aesthetics of the urban environment: Review of the role of vegetation. *Landscape and Urban Planning* 15(1–2): 85–106.

Spirn, A. W. (2005) Restoring Mill Creek: Landscape literacy, environmental justice and city planning and design. *Landscape Research* 30(3): 395–413.

Spitalas N. (2003) *Stratégie de développement d'une ville frontalière grecque.* Université de Nantes.

Stavridis, S. (1990) *The symbolic relationship with space. How social values shape space* (orig. Greek). Publ. Kalvos. Athens.

Stubbs, M. (2008) Natural green space and planning policy: Devising a model for its delivery in regional spatial strategies. *Landscape Research* 33(1): 119–139.

Styliadis, A.D., Konstantinidou, D.G., Tyxola and K.A. (2008) eCAD System Design – Applications in Architecture. *Int. J. of Computers, Communications & Control*, 3(2): 204-214.

Thwaites, K., Helleur, E. and Simkins, I. M. (2005) Restorative urban open space: Exploring the spatial configuration of human emotional fulfillment in urban open space. *Landscape Research* 30(4): 525–547.

Tveit, M., Ode, A. and Fry, G. (2006) Key concepts in a framework for analyzing visual landscape character. *Landscape Research* 31(3): 229–255.

Ulrich, R. S. (1979) Visual landscapes and psychological well-being. *Landscape Research* 4(1): 17–23.

Vyzantiadou, M.A., Avdelas, A.V. and Zafiropoulos S. (2007) The application of fractal geometry to the design of grid or reticulated shell structures. *Computer-Aided Design*. 39 (1): 51-59.

Wilson, K. (2003) Therapeutic landscapes and First Nations peoples: An exploration of culture, health and place. *Health & Place* 9(2): 83-93.

Zafiropoulos S. (2010) Music Box Sounds Bold Music Building. Recall of Senses and Desirable Relations of Spaces, Sounds, Time and Vibes at Renzo Piano's Parco della Musica in Rome. (Edit.) K. Tsoukala, M. Daniel, Ch. Pantelidou. *Postmodern Standpoints* (orig. Greek). Pp.255-270. Publ. Epikentro. Thessaloniki.

Zavraka, D.D. (2007) Haptic Landscapes: Case study of cemeteries. (Edit.) N. Eleftheriadis, A. Styliadis, I. Paliokas. *Proceedings of the International Conference. LANT07. Landscape Architecture and New Technologies*. Pp. 55-67. Department of Landscape Architecture. Technological Educational Institute of Kavala. Drama – Greece.

Websites:

1. http://www.landscape.mmu.ac.uk/news/2005/everton (Everton Park Sensory Garden) (last accessed 12 Feb 2009)

2. http://wapedia.mobi/en/Sensory_garden (last accessed 12 Feb 2009)

3. http://www.sensory-garden.com (last accessed 12 Feb 2009)

4. http://www.hgtv.com/landscaping/sensory-garden-for-the-pacific-northwest (Sensory Garden for the Pacific Northwest) (last accessed 12 Feb 2009)

5. http://www.sensorytrust.org.uk/information/factsheets/sensory_garden1.html (Sensory Garden Design Advice) (last accessed 12 Feb 2009)

6. http://www.ces.purdue.edu/vanderburgh/horticulture/garden4blind.htm (Gardening for the Blind: Tips for People with Impaired Vision) (last accessed 12 Feb 2009)

7. http://www.herbcompanion.com/Gardening/Seeing-with-Other-Senses-Gardens-for-the-Blind.aspx (Seeing with Other Senses: Gardens for the Blind) (last accessed 12 Feb 2009)

8. http://www.bgci.org/resources/article/0140 (Nanjing Botanic Garden - The Largest Botanical Garden for Visually-Handicapped People in China) (last accessed 12 Feb 2009)

9. http://www.abc.net.au/gardening/stories/s1069753.htm (Fact Sheet: Healing Garden) (last accessed 12 Feb 2009)

10. http://land.asla.org/2007/0911/lain.html (American Society of Landscape Architects) (last accessed 12 Feb 2009)

11. http://www.polesworthabbey.heralded.org.uk/?q=node/5 (Sensory Garden) (last accessed 12 Feb 2009)

APPENDIX

Questionnaire

How old are you?
Are you married?
What is the subject of your studies and what is your profession?
What have you dealt with generally in your life?
If one asked you in what social class you belong to, what would you answer?

----

1. What is the landscape you most frequently imagine?
2. Where did you spend your childhood years? What did you like there? How did you imagine this place?
3. How would others describe it? What impressed you most from what you heard?
4. When do you feel relaxed? How do you achieve relaxation?

5. During a walk, in order to feel relaxed would you like to walk barefoot on:

a. wooden floor
b. carpet
c. pebbles
d. grass
e. dry sand
f. wet sand
g. mud
h. puddle
i. other.....

6. When you go on an excursion, where do you usually go?
a. forest
b. beach
c. field-range
d. other..........

7. Were there moments while listening to music that you imagined a landscape? If so what kind of music? What type of landscape? What kind of music do you listen to in general?

8. What is your favourite taste? What does it make you feel when you experience it? What is your mostly unforgettable meal? Do you remember an exquisite taste?

9. With whom do you prefer to go for a walk: a. alone, b. with friends, c. with your family, d. with your life-partner? Where would you like to go (or have you gone) for your honeymoon?

10. What is the most appaling place you have ever visited for a walk? Why?

11. If you decided to move out, where would you like to go?

12. What country would you like to visit if you won a ticket?

13. If you had the possibility to acquire a cottage in a place, what would this place be (mountain, sea, field-range, etc.)

14. If this moment they offered you a house, how would you like this house to be? Would you like a house with a garden? How should the garden be?

15. Would you like to have a park in your neighbourhood? How do you imagine it?

16. What would the perfect park in your neighbourhood look like?

17. How do you imagine the perfect neighbourhood in order to live there, a. alone, b. with your wife, c. with your children?

18. What is your favourite plant and your favourite landscape?

19. If you decided to take up painting, what would you draw? Is there anything you would never draw?

20. Your best friend is a man or a woman? Is he/she blind? Where did you meet him/her?

21. What is your favourite animal? What is your relationship with animals? Do you cuddle them?

INDEX OF CONCEPTS

A
Age 47, 48, 60
Anxiety 50, 47, 69, 74
Aromatic 38, 39, 42, 44, 46, 60, 63, 64

C
City 61, 65, 66

D
Decorative 38, 39, 63, 64
Design 29, 32, 55, 58

E
Education 50-52
Entertainment 35, 36, 53-55, 65-68
Environment
    built 36, 38, 44-46, 50-52, 57, 58, 61, 62, 64, 65
    natural 36

F
Family 58
Fauna 38, 39, 44-47, 61-65
Filter of Perception 23, 24
Flora 44, 45, 57, 61-64
Functionalism 34-36, 47, 48, 53, 65-68

G
Gender 46, 47
Geomorphologic 39, 41, 54, 61, 63

H
Historical 17, 28, 41-43, 60

I
Icon 29-31, 56, 57
Index 29-31, 47, 48, 50, 51, 56, 58
Island 42, 61

L
Landscape
    diversity 54, 55
    Sociology 12, 15, 27
Low vegetation 37, 44, 45, 50-52, 61-64

M
Metaphor 29-31, 56
Monotony, monotonous 49, 50, 55, 60
Monument 29, 41-43, 49
Mountain(-ous) 39, 42, 43
Music 33, 55, 60

N
Networking 48, 65-67
Nostalgia 42, 46, 47, 60

O
Origin 53, 54

P
Park 31, 34, 60, 65
Past 41-43, 60
Pavement 38

R
Residence 35, 36, 53, 54, 65-67
Road 61

S
Senses
    Anthropology of 12, 15
    Combination of 59
Sensory Garden 19, 20
Smell 12, 15, 20, 28, 32-34, 44-46, 54, 58-60
Social class 55-57
Socialisation, socializing 34, 36, 65-67
Semiotics 57
Sound 11, 12, 18, 19, 33, 55, 58, 60, 61
Soundscape 18, 19, 60
Square 28, 30, 38, 47, 61, 65
Symbol 29-31, 47, 56, 58

T
Touch(-ing) 11, 12, 15, 18, 19, 31-34, 38, 41, 43, 45, 59, 60
Trace 29-31, 49-51, 56, 57
Transport 34-36, 51, 52, 65-67
Trees 37
    broad-leaved 38, 39, 45, 62-64
    coniferous 39, 63, 64
    fruit-bearing 39, 62-64

V
Village 43, 54

W
Walking 37, 44, 60, 61
Work 35, 36, 65-67

About the authors:

Ms Angeliki Koskina studied Landscape Architecture at the University of Kavala Institute of Technology, Greece, and specialised in the analysis of non-visual landscape. She also studied Piano, Theory of Music, and Music Therapy at the Mozart Conservatorium of Patra, Greece. She has worked as a musician and composer and participated in several architectural exhibitions. She has published academic papers. Her research interests focus on Music and Landscape, Landscape Sociology, and Anthropology of Senses.

Dr Nikolas Hasanagas studied Forest and Environmental Science at the Aristotle University of Thessaloniki, Greece, and Sociology, Political Science, and Ethnology at the University of Goettingen, Germany. He obtained his PhD in Environmental Policy Analysis at the University of Goettingen. He has published academic papers. He has also been an invited guest speaker and reviewer for international academic journals. His research interests focus on Environmental Policy and Landscape Sociology.

***ibidem*-Verlag**

Melchiorstr. 15

D-70439 Stuttgart

info@ibidem-verlag.de

www.ibidem-verlag.de
www.ibidem.eu
www.edition-noema.de
www.autorenbetreuung.de